So, What Is God's Will?

The Perspective From the Upper Deck!

AMY SCOVIL

WESTBOW°
PRESS
A DIVISION OF THOMAS NELSON
& ZONDERVAN

Author Credits: Thanks to God Almighty and Everlasting!

Scripture taken from the King James Version of the Bible.

WestBow Press books may be ordered through booksellers or by contacting:

WestBow Press
A Division of Thomas Nelson & Zondervan
1663 Liberty Drive
Bloomington, IN 47403
www.westbowpress.com
1 (866) 928-1240

ISBN: 978-1-4908-3249-4 (sc)
ISBN: 978-1-4908-3250-0 (e)

Library of Congress Control Number: 2014905915

Printed in the United States of America.

WestBow Press rev. date: 04/04/2014

Contents

The original intent for this book was a 365 daily devotional study. From college days on I have delved into favorites such as Oswald Chamber's My Upmost For His Highest; Max Lucado's Grace For the Moment; Joni Eareckson Tada's More Precious Than Silver; and My latest; Jesus Calling by Sarah Young. The First Few devotionals I had written for the book...I decided to show my mom one day to see what she thought. Her opinion was favorable except in her words... "What do you mean by that?..." caused me to take a second look. I discovered that one day's devotional was worthy of an entire book.... Hence... "So What is God's Will." came about based on one day's devotional... and a life of taking two steps forward and one step back...Here's what I've learned along the way... With GOD'S book...The BIBLE! I pray it is a source of inspiration and revelation to you.

Original Devotional Entry

SO WHAT IS GOD'S WILL?

Deuteronomy 30:20 That thou mayest love the LORD thy God, and that thou mayest obey his voice, and that thou mayest cleave unto him: for he is thy life, and the length of thy days.

We want know what is God's will for our lives. Where to go to school, who to marry, what job should I take? Short term goals and long term goals alike; we want to be in God's will. So how do we discover what it is? The world is shouting one thing; God speaks different. It is his will that you live! I overheard a Billy Joel song on the radio the other day... "Only the good die young!" If you mean young at heart... OK... if you mean young in age... that is the farthest from the truth. Long lives and good days are the Father's heart. *Exodus 20:12 Honor thy father and thy mother: that thy days may be **long upon the land** which the Lord thy God giveth thee.* My friend, go back to the Word of God and seek his face earnestly in prayer. God's will and his heart for his children is no mystery.

It is his will that you be saved! Read *John 3: 14-17, I Thess. 5:9*
It is his will that you be healed! Read *Psalm 103:3*
It is his will that you have childlike faith! Read *Mark 10:15*
It is his will that you know the goodness of God! Read *Exodus 34:6, Isaiah 63:7*
It is his will that you obey him and hear his voice! Read *Jeremiah 7:23*
It is his will that you conform to the image of Christ! Read *Romans 8:29*
It is his will that you be salt and light! Read *Matthew 5:13-14*
It is his will that you be blessed! Read *Genesis 22:17-18, Ephesians 1:3*
It is his will that you bear fruit! Read *John 15:8, Colossians 1:10*
It is his will that you get wisdom! Read *Proverbs 4:7, Ephesians 1:17*
It is his will that you overcome! Read *Romans 8:35-37, James 1:12*
It is his will that you be safe! Read *Proverbs 11:14, Proverbs 3:23*
It is his will that you walk in the Spirit! Read *Galatians 5:17, 6:8, Ephesians 4:3*
It is his will that you do good works! Read *2 Timothy 3:16-17, 2 Corinthians 9:8*
It is his will that you be sanctified! Read *I Thess. 5:23*
If you've made Jesus your Lord your continual prayer will be... *Luke 22:42 "Lord, not my will, but Yours be done." And... 1 Peter 4:1-2 Because Jesus suffered for me in the flesh, I will arm myself with this same mind that I will no longer live my time in the flesh for the lusts of men, but for the will of God.* A few principles that I recently learned in my Bible Study Fellowship class are to:
1) Pray for wisdom to stay in God's will and know what it is for me. (We accomplish God's will by doing things God's way) and 2) not to presume upon God and put him to the test. Jesus confronted the devil in the wilderness with the WORD *"It is written again, thou shalt not tempt the Lord thy God." Matt 4:7*

Prayer
Dear Lord, Thank you for your desire for me to know you and enjoy you forever. Please grant me wisdom to know your will and to walk in your will for my life. Please help me make choices that draw me closer to you and closer to Heaven each and every day. I will wait for your answers and your timing knowing that you have only the best for me. I trust you Lord. I love you. AMEN

Introduction

Dad and I after
deep sea fishing

When I was 18 I went deep sea fishing with my dad down in Mazatlan, Mexico. For one of us the experience was great. For the other the experience was miserable. The one who had the better of the two experiences was seated on the upper-deck of the boat where he could see the direction the boat was headed. The other was seated on the lower deck and could only see the back end... and when the boat was out to sea and the boat was being rocked that person was throwing up in the latrine the entire trip. When the boat approached it's ending, the bottom dwellers were encouraged..."Keep your eyes on the horizon. And look for the shoreline. Sure enough the land came into view again and when the feet landed on the ground that person never felt better. The person on the top deck, however, spent the entire time enjoying the views from above and even caught a fish!

Why do you think the upper-deck person had the better experience? It is my belief he had a different perspective! He could see the driver of the boat. He could see the direction the boat was headed. He could look all around and gain breathtaking views from every angle. I think our Heavenly Father wants us to have the upper-deck perspective. He's the Captain. The Word is His compass. He says... "I've got great plans for you...I've got a job for you" and so much more. We've got to know that Jesus is not only in our boat, as His disciples, but He also has command of the wind and the waves around the boat.

The BIBLE.... Basic Instructions Before Leaving Earth... is filled with stories so that we get to know just that....the Father's HEART! His desire is for us to know Him, cling to Him, hold His hand, and trust and allow Him to safely carry us home. Not only do we want to know His will but we want to be IN His will for our lives. It's an easy thing in this world to get confused as to just exactly what His will is if we don't know what His Word says. So in order for us to not be deceived we have to be diligent students of His Word... I mean every day.

In this book I'm going to share just a few Scriptures from Gods WORD that express the Father's heart. At the beginning of each day is one Scripture that is highlighted. I encourage you to put this Scripture to memory. This is going to be a journey of exploring and comparing what the WORD of God says to what the world

Says. On the way, you'll be able to write your own comments about what you've seen from past experiences, in the news, and the world around you. Then you will be able to, (after hearing God's opinion), plan and pray for God's vision for your life, future, relationships, finances, and faith! Be prepared with a Bible and pen in hand.

As you study I pray that you will be able to "prove: what is that good, and acceptable, and perfect, will of God." (Romans 12:2)

the upper-deck fisherman ⟶

DAY 1

It's God's Will that you obey Him and Hear His Voice!

Jeremiah 11:4b Obey My voice, and do them (the words of the covenant), according to all which I command you: so shall ye be My people, and I will be your God:

You grow up hearing lots of voices: your parents, your teachers, your employers, your leaders, what's on the TV. What are some of the things spoken (good or bad) that stand out to you regarding your life and future:

_____

_____

_____

_____

_____

One way you can hear the Lords voice is through memorizing Scripture. What Scripture, maybe even the one that led you to reading this book, is in your heart that God has spoken to you:

_____

_____

_____

Write down today's Scripture: Jeremiah 11:4b:

_____

_____

_____

_____

What are some of the commandments God wants us to obey? Let's look at old and new testament Scriptures to find a few. Read Exodus 20 1-17. Write down 5 commandments you just read: 1) _____

2) _____

3) _____

4) _____

5) _____

Now read some New Testament Scripture: Mark 12:29-31

Write down Mark 12:29-31:

_____

_____

_____

_____

_____

Today's lesson: Hearing God's voice and obeying His commands; comes with a promise.... "So shall ye be My people, and I will be your God." What a gift.... God as Father and to be known as His child, right?! It's pretty important, then, that we store up His commands in our hearts and learn to hear His voice!

Just like a tree in nature has deep roots, underground, that no one can see that keeps it standing when the winds blow and the storms come, so we too, have to have our roots deep in God's Word in order to stand strong as Christians.

Write down Jesus's words in Matthew 7:24-25:

_____

_____

_____

_____

_____

_____

_____

Make a declaration for you that you will build your house upon the solid rock of Jesus Christ today: The apostle Paul when speaking of King David in the Old Testament said of David in verse 22 of Acts 13... "And when He (the Lord) raised up unto them David to be their king; to whom also He gave testimony, and said, I have found David the son of Jesse, a man after mine own heart, which shall fulfill all My Will..." Let's pursue, like David, God's heart and watch how God fulfills His Will for our lives!

DAY 1

Prayer: Write your own prayer of commitment to the Lord to seek Him in His Word, obey His commandments, and hear His voice... IT'S HIS WILL FOR YOU!

_____

_____

_____ AMEN!

DAY 2

It's God's Will that you be Safe!

Proverbs 1:33 But whoso hearkeneth unto me shall dwell safely, and shall be quiet from fear of evil.

Have you noticed all the tornados, floods and hurricanes in the news? How about earthquakes and fires? Have you ever been in a car accident? What about all the gun violence? Have you ever taken a risk and done something dangerous? What about a dare from a friend? Seems like trouble is all around isn't it? Write down what you have seen lately and or experienced in your own life.

_____

_____

_____

So what is God's will for you when danger comes and what choices can you make? In His Word God says you can be totally free from fear. Let's look at some scriptures that share who you are in Christ when you make Jesus your Lord.

1 Peter 1: 1-9 Says... "Peter, an apostle of Jesus Christ, to the strangers scattered throughout Pontus, Galatia, Cappadocia, Asia, and Bithynia, Elect according to the foreknowledge of God the Father, through sanctification of the Spirit, unto obedience and sprinkling of the blood of Jesus Christ: Grace unto you, and peace, be multiplied. Blessed be the God and Father of our Lord Jesus Christ, which according to His abundant mercy hath begotten us again unto a lively hope by the resurrection of Jesus Christ from the dead, To an inheritance incorruptible, and undefiled, and that fadeth not away, reserved in heaven for you, Who are kept by the power of God through faith unto salvation ready to be revealed in the last time wherein ye greatly rejoice, though now for a season, if need be, ye are in heaviness through manifold temptations: That the trial of your faith, being much more precious than of gold that perisheth, though it be tried with fire, might be found unto praise and honour and glory at the appearing of Jesus Christ: Whom having not seen, ye love; in whom, though now ye see Him not yet believing, ye rejoice with joy unspeakable and full of glory: Receiving the end of your faith, even the salvation of your souls." Friend, isn't it so good that you are "KEPT by the POWER of GOD!"

One time I was walking down a city street at night returning home from a trip studying at college in the 90s. I was by myself and had so many reasons to be fearful for various dangers that are known in the area. All the sudden, the thought that... I HAD

JESUS... came to mind, and it was like angels were surrounding me. The road beneath me, though it was dark out, appeared heavenly! I knew at that moment that I never needed to be afraid of any one or any thing. God was with me and I was safe with Him. Let's look at some examples in the Old Testament of people who God kept safe and how we can be safe.

Write down Exodus 23:20

_____

_____

_____

Look up and Write down Leviticus 25: 18-19

_____

_____

_____

_____

Notice that it is those who do what is right in God's sight that will receive God's safety.
Let's look at Noah's life.
Read Genesis Chapter 6
Write down Genesis 6:22

_____

_____

NOW read GeNeSiS 7-9

Write doWN your thoughts oN WHy God Saved NoaH From the FLood aNd Write doWN SoMe WayS iN WHicH God bLeSSed NoaH For buiLdiNg the arK.

_____

_____

_____

_____

_____

DoN't you WaNt to MaKe the coMMitMeNt to be iN God'S WiLL For your LiFe iN thiS Matter? It iS God'S deSire to protect you aNd Keep you SaFe. Pray aNd SeeK the Lord For your LiFe... PaSt, PreSeNt, aNd Future. LiKe NoaH, HoW caN you buiLd yourSeLF aNd arK... (WitH JeSuS!) Write aNd Put to MeMory ProverbS 1:33

_____

_____

_____

_____

Day 3

It's God's Will that you be blessed!

Ephesians 1:3 Blessed by the God and Father of our Lord Jesus Christ, who hath blessed us with all spiritual blessings in heavenly places in Christ:

Take a moment to dream. Picture yourself blessed! How? You might ask. Think of every area of your life. Start with your body. Are you well? Are you free from all pain? Do you feel strong and able to accomplish anything? How about your emotions? Are you feeling at peace? Is there joy and laughter in your belly? What about your finances? Is there provision for everything you need, and then some? Do you have enough to store up for your future and freely give to anyone in need? What about your relationships? Do you have people who love you and you can love back? Have you thought about your spiritual life? Are you right with God? Are you happy that Christ forgave your sins on the cross? Write down what some blessings in your life might look like for you.

_____

_____

_____

Now go back to the memory verse and write it down here for you to remember it: Ephesians 1:3 _____

_____

_____

From the very beginning of creation it has been God's desire to bless. When God made Adam He gave Him everything to enjoy, even His presence. And even a wife. And He made them in His image. Genesis 1:28 says... "And God blessed them, and God said unto them, Be fruitful, and multiply, and replenish the earth, and subdue it:" All of it... a gift from God. And God set up one condition. A tree that they could not eat from. A so called... "tree of obedience." This was Adam and Eve's gift back to God... their obedience. Well, Adam and Eve failed and the ground became cursed. But God never failed. He covered Adam and Eve with clothing and He graced them with a promise...JESUS!

For Abraham, years later, God made a promise to Him. God chose Abraham. He loved Him. He revealed Himself to Abraham and asked Abraham to live a life of faith and obedience to God. Abraham did that and God called him righteous. This is what God promised to Abraham in Genesis 22: 17-18. "That in blessing I will bless thee and in multiplying I will multiply thy seed as the stars of the heaven, and as the sand which is upon the sea shore; and thy seed shall possess the gate of his enemies; and in thy seed

Shall all the nations of the earth be blessed; because thou hast obeyed My voice." Has the Lord revealed Himself to you. Then like Abraham, by faith and obedience to God's voice, you can walk in God's blessings.

Moses, another man called by God, met with God face to face on the mountain, and was in charge of relaying God's laws with the Israelites.

Read Deuteronomy Chapter 28 1-14.

WOW! All the blessings which are promised for following God's commands! Write some of the blessings promised here:

_____

_____

_____

Now read Deuteronomy 28 15-68. All the curses for disobedience.

Friend, it is God's heart to bless you. God is a holy and jealous God. From the beginning of time, God planned for Jesus to come and pay the price on behalf of sinful men in order to restore man to God. What a generous God to provide such a gift. His own Son. He wants you blessed!

Day 3

Write down Romans 4:7-8

_____

_____

_____

_____

_____

Standing in Christ's righteousness alone will not only cause you to rejoice but it can effect an entire city! In Proverbs 11:11a God says... "Upright citizens bless a city and make it prosper." (NLV) pretty cool, huh? And write down Proverbs 10:22:

_____

_____

God's desire is to bless you richly and give you great joy, not only in Heaven, but here on earth, too! This is the perspective from the upper-deck: Look at Jesus! The apostle Paul, in writing to Timothy, said this of Him: "Which in His times He shall shew, who is the blessed and only Potentate, the King of kings, and Lord of lords; Who only hath immortality, dwelling in the light which no man can approach unto; (1 Timothy 6:15) Ask the Holy Spirit to reveal Jesus to you. Have you caught one glimpse of His glory? He is your blessing now and in the future! A pastor friend of mine says this... "Keep God first place.... And you'll Never be Last!" Write your prayer of commitment to the Lord Here:

_____

_____

_____

_____

_____

_____

_____

_____ AMeN

Day 4

It's God's Will that you prosper!

PSALM 1:3 And He shall be like a tree planted by the rivers of water, that bringeth forth his fruit in his season; his leaf also shall not wither; and whatsoever he doeth shall prosper.

Just as you learned that God wants to bless you, (for hearkening to His voice and choosing to obey His commandments) God also wants to prosper you. What does prosperity look like? Picture what abundant life would look like to you! Lots of land to own? Lots of houses? Lots of family and friends? Lots of things? A good name?

Seems like contentment is the key. Check out what the apostle Paul says in Philippians 4:10-13... "But I rejoiced in the Lord greatly, that now at the last your care of me hath flourished again; wherein ye were also careful, buy ye lacked opportunity. Not that I speak in respect of want; for I have learned, in whatsoever state I am, therewith to be content. I know both how to be abased, and I know how to abound: everywhere and in all things I am instructed both to be full and to be hungry, both to abound and to suffer need. I can do all things through Christ which strengtheneth me."

Got Jesus? Got everything!

Paul's life was dedicated to ministering the good news to the un-reached and testifying to what God had done in his own life. Seems we could all follow his example.

Let's take a look at what the Bible says about prospering. Look up the following verses and fill in the blank.

- Genesis 24:35 And the LORD hath _____ my master greatly; and he is become great: and he hath given him flocks, and herds, and silver, and gold, and menservants, and maidservants, and camels, and asses.
- Deuteronomy 6:2-3 That thou mightest fear the LORD thy God, to keep all his statutes and his commandments, which I command thee, thou, and thy son, and thy son's son, all therefore, O Israel, and observe to do it; that it may be well with thee, and that ye may _____ mightily, as the Lord God of thy fathers hath promised thee, in the land that floweth with milk and honey.
- Deuteronomy 28:8 The LORD shall command the blessing upon thee in thy storehouses, and in _____ that thou settest thine hand unto; and he shall bless thee in the land which the LORD thy God giveth thee.
- 2 Chronicles 31:9-10 Then Hezekiah questioned with the priests and the Levites concerning the heaps. And Azariah

the chief priest of the house of Zadok answered him, and said, Since the people began to bring the offerings into the house of the LORD, we have had enough to eat, and have left plenty: For the LORD hath _____ his people; and that which is left is this great store.

- 2 Chronicles 31:21 And in every work that he began in the service of the house of God, and in the law, and in the commandments, to seek his God, he did it with all his heart, and _____.

- Proverbs 8:35 For whoso findeth me findeth _____, and shall obtain favour of the LORD.

- Psalm 37:3 Trust in the LORD, and do good; so shalt thou _____ in the land, and verily thou shalt be fed.

- Proverbs 10:22 The _____ of the LORD, it maketh rich, and he addeth no sorrow with it.

- Proverbs 28:25b But he that putteth his _____ in the LORD shall be made fat.

- Proverbs 13:4 The soul of the sluggard desireth, and hath nothing; but the soul of the _____ shall be made fat.

- Proverbs 22:1 A good name is rather to be chosen than great riches, and _____ favour rather than silver and gold.

- Job 36:11 _____ they obey and serve him, they shall spend their days in prosperity, and their years in pleasures.

- Isaiah 52:12 For ye shall not go out with haste, nor go by flight: For the LORD will go before you; and the God of Israel will be your _____.

- Isaiah 54:13 And all thy children shall be taught of the LORD; and great shall be the _____ of thy children.

- Jeremiah 33:6 Behold, I will bring it health and cure, and I will cure them, and will reveal unto them the _____ of peace and truth.

- Zechariah 8:12 For the seed shall be _____; the vines shall give her fruit, and the ground shall give her increase, and the heavens shall give their dew; and I will cause the remnant of this people to possess all these things.

- Here's some New Testament scriptures:

- Romans 8:32 He that spared not his own Son, but delivered him up for us all, how shall he not with him also _____ give us all things?

- Matthew 6:25-33 Therefore I say unto you, Take no thought for your life, what ye shall eat, or what ye shall drink; nor yet for your body, what ye shall put on, Is not the life more than meat, and the body than raiment? Behold the fowls of the air; for they sow not, neither do they reap, nor gather into barns, yet your heavenly Father feedeth them. Are ye not much better than they? Which of you by taking thought can add one cubit unto his stature? And why take ye thought for raiment? Consider the lilies of the field, how they grow; they toil not, neither do they spin; And yet I say unto you, That even Solomon in all his glory was not arrayed like one of these. Wherefore, if God so clothe the grass of the field, which today is, and tomorrow is cast into the oven, shall he not much more clothe you, O ye of little faith? Therefore take no thought, saying, What shall we eat? Or, What shall we drink? Or wherewithal shall we be clothed? For after all these things do the Gentiles seek: For your heavenly Father knoweth that ye have need of all these things, But seek ye _____ the Kingdom of God and his righteousness; and all these things shall be added unto you.

- Matthew 13:23 But he that received seed into the good ground is he that heareth the word, and understand it; which also beareth fruit, and _____, some an hundredfold, some sixty, some thirty.

- Matthew 19:29 And every one that hath forsaken houses, or brethren, or sisters, or father, or mother, or wife, or children, or lands, for my name's sake, shall receive an hundredfold, and shall _____ everlasting life.

- Mark 10:29-30 And Jesus answered and said, Verily I say unto you, There is no man that hath left house, or brethren, or sisters, or father, or mother, or wife, or children or lands, for my sake, and the gospels, But he shall _____ and hundredfold now in this time, houses, and brethren, and sisters, and mothers, and children, and lands, with persecutions: and in the world to come eternal life.

- John 10:10 The thief cometh not, but for to steal, and to kill, and to destroy. I am come that they might _____, and that they might have it more abundantly.

- 3 JOHN 2 Beloved, I wish above all things that thou mayest _____ and be in health, even as thy _____ prospereth.

Your turn. Write out today's Scripture Memory verse above.
PSALM 1:3

_____

_____

_____

One more verse to copy for today.

Write out Joshua 1:7-8 here

_____

_____

_____

_____

_____

_____

After having the opportunity to look at God's Word above and really meditate on it; take a moment to think about your life and how you could apply these Scriptures.

-What have you learned; What will you change? And how can you ask God to help you to prosper now and for your future. Remember... With GOD on your side you can do anything! DREAM

BIG! HE LOVES YOU! Are you loving Him and what HE loves? Can you see God working in your current situation right now? Are you recognizing it and thanking Him? Are there open doors of opportunities for you to boldly lay hold of? Are you walking the straight and narrow JESUS'S way? Are you seeking God as first place in everything? What are you speaking about yourself, your circumstances, your future. Do you hope in God's Word? God wants you to prosper! And most of all... He wants you to shine for the GOSPELS sake and be about His business...A Fisher of Men! THIS IS GOD'S upper-deck perspective.

ASK God to help you see Him, ask Him to reveal Himself to you and pray that you understand where He's trying to minister to your life right now. Remember... IF you've said yes to Jesus in your life then you have the Holy Spirit working mightily in you, through you, and for you.

Write down any new perspectives you have about God... What do you hope to accomplish that's in your heart? IF you delight yourself in the LORD than He will grant you the desires of your heart. PSALM 37:4

Day 4

_____

_____

_____

_____

_____

_____

Day 5

It's God's Will that you get Wisdom!

Ephesians 1:17 That the God of our Lord Jesus Christ, the Father of glory, may give unto you the Spirit of wisdom and revelation in the knowledge of him:

Have you ever asked someone for advice? Who do you turn to and what do you seek for answers? In the decisions you are making on a daily basis who or what is guiding you? What have been some of the results from that "wisdom?" Write down some examples here?

_____

_____

_____

_____.

When Jesus was 12 years old the Bible declared that even He "increased in wisdom and stature, and in favour with God and man." (Luke 2:52) Wow, was Jesus wise! He taught in parables, He discerned men's hearts, He astonished His own hometown even. "And when he was come into his own country, he taught them in their synagogue, insomuch that they were astonished,

23

and said, Whence hath this man this Wisdom, and these mighty works? Is not this the carpenter's son? Is not his mother called Mary? ..."(Matthew 13:54-55a) Jesus is Wisdom!

1 Corinthians 1:24b... "Christ the power of God, and the Wisdom of God." So Jesus is our Wisdom! (1 Co. 1:30)

Write out the above Scripture for you to remember.
Ephesians 1:17 _____

_____

_____

What does this Wisdom look like? Read and Write down James 3:17

_____

_____

_____

_____.

So when you pray and talk to God ...What a better request can you make then to ask for Wisdom. Proverbs 2:6-7 says... "For the Lord giveth Wisdom: out of his mouth cometh knowledge and understanding. He layeth up sound Wisdom for the righteous: he is a buckler to them that walk uprightly." Solomon did, and read how God was so pleased with his request that he granted him not only Wisdom and knowledge but riches, wealth, and honor. Read 2Chronicles 1:7-12.

So you are blessed if you get wisdom! It will keep you, it's better than rubies; and all the things that may be desired are not to be compared to it. (Proverbs 8:11) Your sleep will be sweet, you will be safe, wisdom adds life to your soul, and grace to your neck! (Proverbs 3:21-24). God calls it the principal thing!

So what are the results of wisdom? Let's study Proverbs and find out! Look up these Scriptures and fill in the blank.

1) Proverbs 3:35 The wise shall inherit _____: but shame shall be the promotion of fools.

2) Proverbs 9:11-12 The years of your life shall be _____.

3) Proverbs 19:8 He that getteth wisdom _____ his own soul; he that keepeth understanding shall find _____.

4) Proverbs 24:3 Through wisdom a _____ is built; and by understanding it is _____.

5) Proverbs 24:14 So shall the knowledge of wisdom by unto thy soul: when thou hast found it, then there shall be a _____, and thy expectation shall not be cut off.

6) Proverbs 28:26 He that trusteth in his own heart is a fool; but whoso walketh wisely, he shall be _____.

7) Ecclesiastes 7:12 For wisdom is a _____, and money is a defence: but the excellency of knowledge is, that _____ giveth _____ to them that have it.

AS Christians, We accomplish God's Will by doing things God's Way. Friend, that takes Wisdom! Won't you pray for God's Wisdom for every situation and person you encounter? Make a life-long commitment to growing in Wisdom. One suggestion for reading Proverbs is to read one chapter a day per Month. There are 31 proverbs and 31 days in a Month so you can read and re-read all throughout the year. In My life, I've learned that I need fresh Wisdom for every situation I face. That means a continual seeking the Lord alone in prayer and hearing the Word and applying it to My life. A revelation you learned two years ago may be true but what truth does Jesus want you to know about Him for the current situation you're facing? Write your prayer here and ask God to help you grow:

_____

_____

_____

_____

_____ AMEN!

Day 6

It's God's Will that you Know the Goodness of God!

2 Peter 1:2-3 Grace and peace be multiplied unto you through the knowledge of God, and of Jesus our Lord, According as his divine power hath given unto us all things that pertain unto life and godliness, through the knowledge of him that hath called us to glory and virtue:

So what thoughts come into your mind when you think of your earthly Father? Is or was he warm and available? Or distant and cold? A communicator or closed-off? No matter how perfect or imperfect your earthly Father is... your Father God in Heaven is incomparably above and beyond anything you could hope, think, or imagine!

Just how good is he? He's so good that he made you and called you good... and desires to share his own goodness with you with the high calling of giving you the gift of his Son, his Spirit, and a future with him in Heaven! Just listen to his heart in Matthew 7:11. "If ye then, being evil, know how to give good gifts unto your children, how much more shall your Father which is in heaven give good things to them that ask Him?" God is a giver and His heart is to be good to you!

Write out today's memory verse at the top: 2nd Peter 1:2-3

_____

_____

_____

_____

_____

God's ultimate gift was His own Son on the cross. 2 Corinthians 5:21 says... "For He hath made Him to be sin for us, who knew no sin; that we might be made the righteousness of God in Him." Because of Jesus we can experience His righteousness, His peace, and His goodness. What a good God! To take what we couldn't do for ourselves and put it on Himself! Basically He's saying... "Let me handle this for you. I can take care of this for you... I love you!" How gracious! In return we are His goodness to others!

Have you ever been given a 2nd chance before? I mean when you've gone to do something, and in the middle of it you just botched the whole thing up? When I was in high school I had a job at the Dairy Queen, my first job. Well, I really liked the buster bars. I got to liking them so much that I started sneaking bars from the freezer and taking a few bites out of them... basically stealing. Well that went on for a while until I got caught red-handed. I was told to wait upstairs to have a conversation with my manager. I was so ashamed of myself. Well you know what my manager did? He didn't fire me... He gave me a second chance! Boy, was I relieved. A few months later he started an employee of the month program. The person who is chosen employee of the month gets their picture on the wall. Well, I experienced a major turn-around at the second chance given to me... guess whos name and picture was on the wall... Mine! All because my boss was so gracious and gave me a 2nd chance. I had a new heart when I could have been fired. When I was about to leave for college do you know what he did? He sent me off to college with one hundred dollars in my pocket. That was the Lord's favor to me.

See God really believes in us. He longs to be good to us... even to promote us! God gave the Israelites a second chance when Moses was their leader in the desert. While Moses was away on the mountain with God the Israelites sinned. They asked Aaron to make gods out of their gold. Aaron did and when Moses returned with the Ten Commandments from God he found the Israelites naked and carousing around this gold calf. Moses, the Lord's servant, said "Whoever is on the Lords side gather around me." The Levites did and the rest died by the sword. About three thousand people.

Well God gave those Israelites a second chance. Moses went back up the mountain and was given the Ten Commandments again. And there the Lord passed before Moses declaring His name... Exodus 34:6-7 "And the Lord passed by before Him, and proclaimed, The Lord, the Lord God, merciful and gracious, longsuffering, and abundant in goodness and truth, Keeping mercy for thousands, Forgiving iniquity and transgression and sin, and that will by no means clear the guilty:"

Friend, has God been good to you? Have you acknowledged that it's God's mouth speaking goodness toward you and His hand performing that goodness? Then give Him glory for it, worship Him, and remember His lovingkindness to you. Keep a record of what the Lord has done, tell about it, it's your story of His goodness toward you. It's worth remembering!

Write your personal record of God's goodness towards you here: (you probably don't have enough room even in this book to contain it all)

_____

_____

_____

_____

Isaiah 63:7 I will mention the lovingkindnesses of the LORD, and the praises of the LORD, according to all that the LORD hath bestowed on us, and the great goodness toward the house of

Israel, which he hath bestowed on them according to his mercies, and according to the multitude of his lovingkindnesses.

Always keep God's upper-deck perspective in mind as you journey through this life: God longs, yearns, even looks for ways to be good to you. He loves you so much! If you're still not convinced read the story of the prodigal son...Luke 15!

Make a commitment to remember, recount, and retell all God's goodness towards you all your days:

_____

_____

_____

_____

_____

_____

_____

Day 7

It's God's Will that you be Healed!

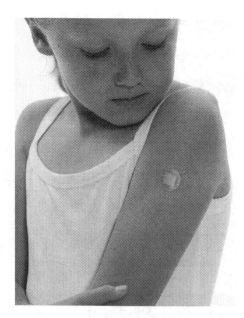

PSALM 103 Bless the Lord, O My Soul, and Forget Not all His benefits: Who Forgiveth all thine iniquities; Who Healeth all thy diseases:

Have you ever thought about the amazing way God made us. Your skin for example... What happens when you get a cut? Well, you put a band-aid on and watch it heal back together!

Have you ever been healed of something? Anything? Write it down. Do you need a healing? Write it down here.

_____

_____

How do I know that it's God's Will that you be healed? Because God sent Jesus and Jesus is healing. The Healer Himself, took our sicknesses and diseases upon His back on the cross. 1 Peter 2:24 says... "Who His own self bare our sins in being dead to sins, should live unto righteousness; by whose stripes ye were healed." Jesus is the source of your healing! Before He went to the cross Luke, the physician, one of Jesus disciples mentions in Luke 6:19

33

"And the whole multitude sought to touch him; for there went virtue out of him, and healed them all."

During Jesus's ministry on earth his heart is clearly expressed. Just listen to the story of the leprous man.

Matthew 8 1-4 "When he was come down from the mountain, great multitudes followed him. And behold, there came a leper and worshipped him, saying, Lord, if thou wilt, thou canst make me clean. And Jesus put forth his hand, and touched him, saying, I will; be thou clean. And immediately his leprosy was cleansed." Like the leprous man have you worshipped the Lord and asked for a healing if you need it? Jesus says... "I am willing." Do you believe it?

Go ahead and write today's introduction verse above: Psalm 103

_____

_____

The leprous man worshipped the Lord. Look what the centurion did when he sought Jesus for healing. Matthew 8:5-8

"And when Jesus was entered into Capernaum, there came unto him a centurion, beseeching him, and saying, Lord, my servant lieth at home sick of the palsy, grievously tormented. And Jesus saith unto him, I will come and heal him. The centurion answered and said, Lord, I am not worthy that thou shouldest come under my roof; but speak the word only, and my servant shall be healed."

Think of the attitude of the centurion. The Bible says he "beseeched" the Lord. What does that mean? It means to beg urgently. Then he says... "I'm not worthy to have you come under my roof; but speak the word only." The centurion had a humble heart. Jesus honored his faith and his prayers were answered.

Another attitude the centurion had was love for his servant who was sick. He had compassion on him just as Jesus had compassion.

Your attitude matters to Jesus! Look at Isaiah 57:15 "For thus saith the high and lofty One that inhabiteth eternity, whose name is Holy; I dwell in the high and holy place, with him also that is of a contrite and humble spirit, to revive the spirit of the humble, and to revive the heart of the contrite ones." Jesus is a humble King. When he went to the cross and was being crucified, mocked, and beaten he didn't only defend himself he prayed and said, "Father, forgive them; for they know not what they do."

Check out the two attitudes that Jesus compares in Luke 18:1-14.

"And he spake this parable unto certain which trusted in themselves that they were righteous, and despised others; Two men went up into the temple to pray; the one a Pharisee, and the other a publican. The Pharisee stood and prayed thus with himself, God, I thank thee, that I am not as other men are, extortioners, unjust, adulterers, or even as this publican. I fast twice in the week, I give tithes of all that I possess. And the publican, standing afar off, would not lift up so much as his eyes unto heaven, but smote upon his breast, saying, God be merciful to me a sinner. I tell you, this man went down to his house justified rather than the other; For every one that exalteth himself shall be abased; and he that humbleth himself shall be exalted." Attitude matters to God! What do you boast about? Where is your heart? How do you see yourself? Where is your confidence?

God is most merciful and his desire for us is that we sow seeds of mercy. Do you need healing? Are you praying for someone who needs healing? The Bible says that if you are a disciple of Jesus Christ then in Jesus name you are able to lay hands on the sick, and they shall recover. Mark 16:18 Write your prayers to the Lord here:

_____

_____

_____

_____

_____

_____

Day 8

It's God's Will that you be Saved!

I Thesselonians 5:8-9 But let us, who are of the day, be sober, putting on the breastplate of faith and love; and for a helmet, the hope of salvation. For God hath not appointed us to wrath, but to obtain salvation by our Lord Jesus Christ who died for us, that, whether we wake or sleep, we should live together with him.

So have you ever wondered... "Why am I here?" Have you ever felt loaded down by personal successes or failures, or the troubles of the world and just felt like life was meaningless? Have you searched for meaning in position or power, in material goods or money? So have you asked yourself... "Where can I turn? To whom can I turn? How can I be saved from it all? And where am I going?" Have you known that God was real and you were hungry for a deeper relationship but didn't know how to pursue one? Take comfort, friend. God's got a plan for you for good and not for harm. (Jeremiah 29:11) And his plan for you is to see you saved! Your job is to believe, trust and rejoice in it! Let's explore this some more. Rewrite today's memory verse above...

_____

_____

_____

_____

So How does this plan work? We are called by God to Hear the good news of salvation... We witness it in God's word and then we respond. John 3: 15-17 That whosoever believeth in Him should not perish, but have eternal life. For God so loved the world, that He gave His only begotten Son, that whosoever believeth in Him should not perish, but have everlasting life. For God sent not His Son into the world to condemn the world; but that the world through Him might be saved." These verses tell us that if we believe Jesus as the scriptures say... than we will have life everlasting. For Jesus says, "I am the way, the truth, and the life. No one comes to the Father but through Me." John 14:6... WHAT A GIFT! And we know that it's not anything we could achieve on our own! Look up and write down Ephesians 2: 8-9

_____

_____

So if we can't earn it How should we respond?

1) We can pay careful attention to it! Hebrews 2:3 "How shall we escape, if we neglect so great salvation; which at the

First began to be spoken by the Lord, and was confirmed unto us by them that heard him;" Read and write down Philippians 2:12

_____

_____

_____

Alone time with God in word and prayer, Fellowship with other believers, growing in the church.... All important.

2) REJOICE IN YOUR SALVATION! When the Israelites were delivered out of Egypt they SANG unto the Lord... EXODUS 15:2 "The Lord is my strength and song, and he is become my salvation; he is my God, and I will prepare him an habitation; my Father's God, and I will exalt him." Write down what Hannah did when she won her victory in the Lord 1 Samuel 2:1

_____

_____

_____

PSALM 62:2 He only is my rock and my salvation; he is my defence; I shall not be greatly moved.

3) Talk about GOD'S SALVATION! The good news of Jesus Christ is the most contagious gospel in the world! The Lord says

IN PSALM 50:23 WHOSO OFFERETH PRAISE GLORIFIETH ME: AND TO HIM THAT ORDERED HIS CONVERSATION ARIGHT WILL I SHOW THE SALVATION OF GOD. GOD'S UNSPEAKABLE GIFT, HIS SON JESUS, SHOULD ALWAYS BE ON OUR LIPS. PRAISE HIM IN THE MORNING, IN THE EVENING, IN THE IN-BETWEEN TIME. LIFT HIM HIGH, SET HIM BEFORE YOU, TRUST HIM, AND LET HIM LEAD YOU TO SPEAK OF HIM TO OTHERS!

THE great evangelist of the 21 century, Billy Graham, just completed a nation-wide telecast on his 95th birthday. The title of his message... "The Reason For My Hope...Salvation!" The message's focus was the cross of Christ. What Jesus did for you and His transforming power in your life, because of the cross, never cease to declare it! You can't find this anywhere else. Write out Galations 6:14

_____

_____

_____

PSALM 145:5-7 I WILL SPEAK OF THE GLORIOUS HONOUR OF THY MAJESTY, AND OF THY WONDROUS WORKS. AND MEN SHALL SPEAK OF THE MIGHT OF THY TERRIBLE ACTS; AND I WILL DECLARE THY GREATNESS. THEY SHALL ABUNDANTLY UTTER THE MEMORY OF THY GREAT GOODNESS, AND SHALL SING OF THY RIGHTEOUSNESS.

So I guess I should ask you... Have you had an encounter with the cross of Christ? If not read the book of Mark. Knowing it's God's Will that you be saved How will you live for Him?

_____

_____

_____

_____

Day 9

It's God's Will that you be Sanctified!

1 Thessalonians 5:23 And the very God of peace sanctify you wholly; and I pray God your whole spirit and soul and body be preserved blameless unto the coming of our Lord Jesus Christ.

Has Jesus washed you of your sins? _____

Maybe you had a bad habit, or any sin separating you from your Holy God, and because of His covenant with you, you were cleansed? From the inside out... could you tell?

So what does sanctification mean anyway? Well, I looked up the word "sanctify" in Miriam's Webster dictionary and its meaning is... "to make holy; to consecrate" the second definition is... "to free from sin." You see, God is Holy. And when sin entered the garden with Adam and Eve, it caused them to be separated from God. God didn't leave them alone however. And throughout the Bible we see God, a Holy God, encountering man again and again. God's goal is to sanctify you. Write today's scripture above for memory. 1 Thessealonians 5:23

_____

_____.

In the Old Testament, the use of animal sacrifice was the provision to cleanse from sins... a foreshadowing of what Jesus did in the New Testament once and for all. When God delivered the Israelites out of the hand of the Egyptians, and led them into the wilderness, he instructed them there on how the priest was to be prepared for service. Exodus 29:21 And thou shalt take of the blood that is upon the altar, and of the anointing oil, and sprinkle it upon Aaron, and upon his garments, and upon his sons, and upon the garments of his sons with him: and he shall be hallowed, and his garments, and his sons, and his sons' garments with him." Not only did he prepare the priests but he prepared the tabernacle where they would encounter the Lord. Ch. 29:43 "And there I will meet with the children of Israel, and the tabernacle shall be sanctified by my glory."

In 2 Chronicles 7:15-16 we find Solomon David's son finishing the temple that David his father had planned for the Lord. The Lord's glory filled the house and this is what the Lord says to Solomon... vs.15-16 "Now mine eyes shall be open, and mine ears attent unto the prayer that is made in this place. For now have I chosen and sanctified this house, that my name may be there forever: and mine eyes and mine heart shall be there perpetually.

In the New Testament, before Jesus went to the cross while praying he says in John 17:15-19 "I pray not that thou shouldest take them out of the world, but that thou shouldest keep them

FROM the evil. They are not of the world, even as I am not of the world. Sanctify them through thy truth: thy word is truth. As thou hast sent me into the world, even so have I also sent them into the world. And for their sakes I sanctify myself, that they also might be sanctified through the truth." Jesus's death and resurrection made the way for us to be sanctified! Copy Hebrews 10:10 Here: _____

_____

_____

Just look at what Jesus told the apostle Paul as he called him to his ministry to the Gentiles in Acts 26:17-18 "Now I send thee, To open their eyes, and to turn them from darkness to light, and from the power of satan unto God, that they may receive forgiveness of sins, and inheritance among them which are sanctified by faith that is in me."

So you see by faith in Jesus and the power of the Holy Spirit working within, Christ makes you presentable to God. Romans 15:16 says "That I should be the minister of Jesus Christ to the Gentiles, ministering the gospel of God, that the offering up of the Gentiles might be acceptable, being sanctified by the Holy Ghost."

Don't you just want to give God thanks for his cleansing power on the cross and the working of the Holy Spirit within you making you in right standing with the Father?! 1 Corinthians 6:17 says... "He that is joined unto the Lord is one Spirit." It is God's will that He be intimately involved with your life! Acts 17:28 says... "For in Him (Christ) we live, and move, and have our being;"

Knowing this how will you choose to live your life? What will you do with your body? How will you spend your time? Would you like to be a vessel of honor unto God? Write out 2 Timothy 2:21 _____

_____

_____

Take a moment to invite the Holy Spirit in and pray.

_____

_____

Acts 20:32 And now, brethren, I commend you to God, and to the Word of His grace, which is able to build you up, and to give you an inheritance among all them which are sanctified.

Day 10

It's God's Will that you Walk in the Spirit!

Ephesians 1:13-14 In whom ye also trusted, after that ye heard the word of truth, the gospel of your salvation: in whom also after that ye believed, ye were sealed with that Holy Spirit of promise, Which is the earnest of our inheritance until the redemption of the purchased possession, unto the praise of his glory.

When I was in high school I was involved with almost everything. Cheerleading, Honor Society, Key Club, Leadership, AP classes, and... a part-time job. What I didn't realize was that a prayer at the dinner table and the Lord's Prayer before bed regularly that happened in the years prior, had a lasting impact that led to such fruitful activity. In Fact, When I went to bed at night I was so exhausted from the days' activities I would fall asleep with maybe the first few words of the Lord's Prayer in mind and fall fast asleep. What was at work on the INSIDE, however, without me even realizing it.... was the HOLY SPIRIT finishing those prayers! You see... I had made a public confession of my faith in Christ years earlier. Because I had confessed Jesus as my Lord and Savior the Bible says God freely gave me His Spirit.

(1JOHN 4:13) It also says in Romans 8:26 Likewise the Spirit also helpeth our infirmities: For we know not what we should pray for as we ought: but the Spirit itself maketh intercession for us with groanings which cannot be uttered. And so, what does the Holy Spirit do?

Let's investigate the power of the Holy Spirit at work in our lives.

Look up each Scripture in your Bible and fill in the blanks.

1) Luke 4:1 And _____ being full of the _____ returned from _____, and was led by the Spirit into the wilderness.

2) Luke 4:14 And _____ returned in the _____ of the _____ into Galilee: and there went out a fame of him through _____ the region round about.

3) John 3:8 The wind bloweth where it listeth, and thou hearest the sound thereof, but canst not tell whence it cometh, and whither it goeth: _____

4) John 3:34 For he whom _____ hath sent _____ the _____ of God: For God _____ not the _____ by measure _____.

5) John 4:24 _____ is a _____: and they that _____ him must worship _____ in _____ and _____.

6) JOHN 6:63 It is the _____ that _____: the FLESH profited _____: the words that I speak unto you, they are _____, and they are Life.

7) JOHN 7: 37 In the last day, that great day of the Feast, Jesus stood and cried, saying, If any man _____, let him come unto Me, and _____. He that _____ on Me, as the Scripture hath said, out of his _____ shall flow _____ of living water.

8) JOHN 14:26-27 But the _____, which is the _____, whom the Father will send in My name, he shall teach you _____, and bring _____ things to your _____, whatsoever I have said unto you. _____ I leave with you, My peace I give unto you: not as the _____ giveth, give I unto you. Let not your _____ be _____, neither let it be _____.

9) JOHN 9:26 But when the _____ is come, whom I will send unto you from the Father, even the Spirit of _____, which proceeded from the Father, he shall _____ of Me: And ye also shall bear _____, because ye have been with Me from the _____.

10) Mark 1:8 I indeed have baptized you with _____: but He shall baptize you with the _____ _____.

So you see it's God's will that His good Free Spirit reveal Jesus to you, fill your soul, and empower you to testify to His name.

49

Day 10

Read and Write down Ephesians 1:13-14 here.

_____

_____

_____

Glory to GOD! When you trust Christ, you are Sealed for the day of redemption and you are Christ's bought treasure!

Not only are you Sealed but you are UNITED to the Lord and one Spirit with Him. That's one intimate relationship between you and the Almighty! God's Spirit in you! The power of the Spirit was so strong on the prophet Elijah in the Old Testament that God empowered him to even run faster than a chariot to overtake Ahab! (1 Kings 18:46) Elijah was God's Spokesman in the will of the Lord. When the Lord Says that you can do all things through Christ Who strengthens you... He's talking about His SPIRIT in you to do it is strong!

So back to High School

Besides and behind all this fruitful activity I was involved in was this deep inner need to belong. Being raised by a single mom and not attending church anywhere I found my identity in my relationships at school. My escape from my own broken heart was to turn to weekend partying with all my friends where I found alcohol easily at reach. I drank to the point of sickness the next morning and

Not remembering what I said or did the night before. How scary! I think back and see what dangers the Lord saved me from... For the Scripture says in Ephesians 5:18 "And be not drunk with wine, wherein is excess; but be filled with the Spirit;" because of His grace and as a part of His careful plan of salvation for my life... He had something greater in store I was about to find out my first year of college.

Let's look up some more Scriptures.

1) Acts 1:8 But ye shall receive power, after that the _____ _____ is come upon you: and ye shall be _____ unto me both in _____, and in all Judea, and in Samaria, and unto the _____ part of the _____.

2) And when the day of _____ was fully come, they were _____ with _____ _____ in _____ place.

3) Acts 2:17 And it shall come to pass in the _____ days, saith God, I will pour out of my _____ upon _____ flesh: and your sons and your daughters shall _____, and you're young men shall see _____ and your old men shall dream _____.

4) Acts 8:15-17 Who, when they were come down, prayed for them, that they might receive the _____: (For as yet he was fallen upon none of them: only they were baptized in the name

OF THE _____ _____.) THEN laid they their hands on them, and they _____ the _____.

5) Acts 6:3 Wherefore, brethren, look ye out among you seven men of _____, full of the _____ _____ and _____, whom we may appoint over this _____.

6) Acts 13:52 And the _____ were filled with _____, and with the _____ _____.

So back to college

It was my first year at college and there were many roads that were being exposed to me that I could walk down. Not only career and relationship choices but moral paths as well. Thankfully, at just the right time the Lord grabbed a hold of my older brother who invited me to a college gathering at a church one Tuesday night. On that very night the presence of the Lord was so evident. The atmosphere was electric with joy and I was soon about to find out why. We worshipped the Lord together and I heard the good news. JESUS came to repair the breech between God and my sin. And not only was it at the hightest cost of his death on the cross. (For... "God made him who had no sin to be sin for us, so that in him we might become the righteousness of God." (NIV)) But He rose from the grave and is ALIVE! Everything that I learned as a child suddenly QUICKENED in my spirit. We received communion that night and I knew it was my decision of commitment to the

Lord. As soon as I made that decision in my heart the Holy Spirit came over me in such a powerful way... the weight of my past sins, the weight of others sins, and the worries of the world were lifted. God had kept His covenant and had made that moment just for me. Thank you Jesus for your power to save! Everything was different from that moment on. One thing that I noticed was that I even drove differently. I was a road rager in high school always having to be in the fast lane and God softened me and turned me into a children's church van driver. :) Who knew! All the glory to God! The Holy Spirit began to show me JESUS and I was changed by His love. Shortly after I began my own journey of testifying to the power of the cross.

Let's investigate further.... Use your Bible and fill in the blanks.

7) ROMANS 8:1 There is therefore now no _____ to them which are in _____, who walk not after the _____, but after the _____.

8) ROMANS 8:14-15 For as many as are _____ by the _____ of God, they are the _____ of _____. For ye have not _____ the _____ of _____ again to _____; but ye have received the Spirit of _____, whereby we cry, _____, _____.

9) ROMANS 12:10-11 Be kindly _____ one to another with _____; in honour preferring one another;

Not slothful in business; _____ in _____;
serving the _____;

So after that encounter with the Lord the Holy Spirit began revealing His wisdom to me with all sorts of experiences of Him in nature... Walking down the street, driving in my car, and even sitting quietly before Him at 5 in the morning. I rejoiced that He was my light, my rock, the lifter of my head, and I was His child! My eyes were beholding Him in His beauty and I no longer worried about myself. All's I could see was His love and desired to serve Him with everything. Do you have the upper-deck perspective of being led by God's Spirit?.... Not pursuing the lusts of the flesh... and free (by walking in the presence of His grace) from the law that leads to sin and death?

A Few More Scriptures

9) 2 Corinthians 7:1 Having therefore these _____, dearly _____, let us cleanse ourselves from all _____ of the flesh and _____, perfecting _____ in the fear of God.

10) Galatians 5:16 This I say then, _____ in the Spirit, and ye shall not _____ the _____ of the _____.

11) Galatians 5:25 If we live in the _____ let us also _____ in the Spirit.

12) Galatians 5:5 For we through the _____ wait for the
_____ of _____ by _____.

It is the Lord's will is that you are filled with His Spirit! He want's to empower you for every good work. His desire for you is to be filled with His love, joy, peace, goodness, faith, gentleness, and self-control. That is the fruit of HIS good free spirit to which against these things there is no law. (Galatians 5:22-23) This is your confidence. Can you recognize the Holy Spirit in you comforting you, encouraging you, assuring you of His peace and presence? Empowering you for the days' tasks ahead of you? I love Psalm 4:4 which says... "Stand in awe, and sin not: commune with your own heart upon your bed, and be still." Know that the Holy Spirit is a person who is intimately acquainted with you. Your best friend. The only one who knows everything about you. Nobody on this earth can compare. That's one special relationship. The Bible says He is the one who will never leave you or forsake you. He's in you and He's worth listening to! He's praying for you, interceding on your behalf, working in you... transforming you in your inner man so you become more like Jesus each and every day. This is God's upper-deck perspective. Do you want to live by it? Do you believe it? Do you commit to listening to Him throughout your life no matter where you are and seeking His voice, direction, and will for you? The Spirit's call will always take you along the higher road that leads you to divine life and love and produces fruit in you that lasts. Where the Spirit is there is peace, love, and joy... It's the gift in you. Stir it up! "Oh bless the Lord, Oh My Soul, and all that is within Me. Who Forgives all iniquities, heals all diseases, delivers From destruction, crowns with love and kindness, Fills My Mouth with good things and renews My youth as the eagles." Psalm 103

Write your prayer here:

_____

_____

_____

_____

_____

_____

_____

_____

_____

_____ AMEN

Day 11

It's God's Will that you be Salt, Light, and do good Works!

Matthew 5:16 Let your light so shine before men, that they may see your good works, and glorify your Father which is in heaven.

So, think for a moment about why you might use salt?

_____

_____

Not only is salt used to flavor but also as a preservative to prevent meat from decaying. Have you ever found that it makes you thirsty, too? HMMM

Have you ever thought of yourself as salt? In this world we live in ....God says you are! If you are a disciple of Christ catch this in Matthew 5:13 "Ye are the salt of the earth: but if the salt have lost his savour, wherewith shall it be salted: it is thenceforth good for nothing, but to be cast out, and to be trodden under foot of men."

As a Christian, filled with the Holy Spirit, you are "flavoring" (like salt) your surroundings around you no matter where you are.

Are you encountering someone who is rude, unkind, or hostile? Season with salt! Does one of your sisters or brothers in the Lord need some encouraging? Season with salt! Your words and actions count in every way.

Copy Colossians 4:6 here:

_____

_____

_____

So what does light do?

_____

_____

Not only does it reveal hidden dangers but it points the way and gives guidance! As a disciple of Christ you are the Light of the World! Check out Matthew 5:14-16... "Ye are the light of the world. A city that is set on an hill cannot be hid. Neither do men light a candle, and put it under a bushel, but on a candlestick; and it giveth light unto all that are in the house. Let your light so shine before men that they may see your good works, and glorify your Father which is in heaven."

Let your light shine for Jesus!

God also has good works in store for you!

HOW? The Lord working in us, through us, and for us... living with integrity and sharing the good news of the gospel as we go about our every day lives where the Lord has assigned us by His grace through faith alone.

Copy Ephesians 2:10 here:

_____

_____

_____

This scripture is God's upper-deck perspective for you. This is what you were created for... belonging to Christ, brought nigh by His precious blood, at peace with God, and a member of God's household.

Some Scriptures For Further Study:

1) 2nd Corinthians 9:8 And God is _____ to make all _____ abound toward you: that ye, always having all sufficiency in _____ things, may abound to every _____ work.

2) 1 Peter 2:15 For so is the _____ of God, that with _____ ye may put to silence the _____ of foolish men:

3) Hebrews 10:24 And let us consider one another to provoke unto _____ and to _____ works:

4) Titus 2:7 In all things shewing thyself a pattern of _____ _____: in doctrine shewing _____, gravity, _____.

5) Titus 2:13-14 Looking for that _____ hope, and the _____ appearing of the great God and our Saviour _____ _____: Who gave himself for us, that he might _____ us from _____ iniquity, and _____ unto himself a peculiar _____, _____ of _____ _____.

6) Titus 3:5-8 Not by works of righteousness which we have done, but according to his _____ he saved us, by the washing of regeneration, and renewing of the _____ _____: Which he shed on us abundantly through _____ _____ our Saviour; That being justified by his _____, we should be made heirs according to the _____ of eternal _____. This is a faithful saying, and these things I will that thou affirm constantly, that they which have believed in God might be careful to _____ good works. These things are good and _____ unto men.

7) 2 Timothy 3:16-17 All _____ is given by _____ of God, and is profitable for doctrine, for _____, for _____, for _____ in righteousness: That the man of God may be perfect, thoroughly furnished unto all _____.

So friend, I've learned that God is not asking us for what we don't have.... (If you're hoping for that powerball 5 billion dollar win to do something great for God... fat chance it'll happen) but what God does want is what we do have: the blessings and God-given talents and resources to bless others in our paths right before us: Have you found some success in doing something well? Can you share that gift with someone else? Are you doing your best in your current school or workplace? Have you been blessed financially? Are you sharing it? Are you a beacon of hope and light to all you come across... Even when you're in a tough relationship or circumstance? Then know that you are reflecting God's love, salt, light, and goodness to the world around you. Shine Christian shine!

Spend some time reflecting on what God has brought you through, (even trials-where you've come out on the other side), successes, talents, and God-given vision and ideas for making this world a better place where you can shine today and even dream for a better tomorrow. Thank God for his provision and ask him to help you walk it out and stay the course.

Day 12

It's God's Will that you bear Fruit!

John 15:8 Herein is My Father glorified, that ye bear MUCH Fruit; so shall ye be My disciples.

So what would you rather have?

I've been trying to keep plants in My apartment and I've noticed that I take more delight in the ones that produce flowers and blossoms than the ones whose leaves are browning and not producing any fruit.

With our Heavenly Father, in John 15:8 Jesus actually compares us to trees and says that God is glorified when we, his children, bear fruit. What fruit, you may ask? Back up to verse 7... "If ye abide in Me, and My words abide in you, ye shall ask what ye will, and it shall be done unto you." and back up to verse 4... "Abide in Me, and I in you. As the branch cannot bear fruit of itself,

except it abide in the vine; no more can ye, except ye abide in Me. Verse 5... "I am the vine, ye are the branches: He that abideth in

Me, and I in Him, the same bringeth forth much fruit; for without Me ye can do nothing. And verse 16... "Ye have not chosen Me, but I have chosen you, and ordained you, that ye should go and bring forth fruit, and that your fruit should remain; that whatsoever ye shall ask of the Father in My name, He may give it you.

That's a lot to think about and meditate on! I encourage you to read all of John chapter 15. Luke 6:43 also talks about fruit.... "For a good tree bringeth not forth corrupt fruit; neither doth a corrupt tree bring forth good fruit." And verse 44a "For every tree is known by his own fruit."

Let's investigate for further study!

Write down Colossians 1:10

_____

_____

_____

Philippians 4:17

_____

_____

Here's some Old Testament Scriptures to know:
Write down Genesis 1:28

_____

_____

_____

_____

_____

_____

_____

Leviticus 26:9

_____

_____

_____

Jeremiah 23:3

_____

_____

_____

So you see... it's God's Will that ripe, succulent, delicious fruit come forth from you. Are you using your God given talents to further Heaven on Earth? How are your words to others? Are they kind and truthful? What about your actions towards others? Are you loving? Are you sowing good seeds? ...Are you experiencing joy? Verse 11 of John 15 says... "These things have I spoken unto you, that My joy Might remain in you, and that your joy Might be FULL! So Christian... BE FRUITFUL in JESUS NaMe!

Here's your opportunity to ask the Lord to make you Fruitful For every good work. Write it doWN and Watch hoW He answers this prayer doWN the road For you. You can do it!

_____

_____

_____

_____

_____

_____

_____

_____

_____ AMEN!

Day 13

It's God's Will that you overcome!

Revelation 2:17 He that hath an ear, let him hear what the Spirit saith unto the churches; To him that overcometh will I give to eat of the hidden manna, and will give him a white stone, and in the stone a new name written, which no man knoweth saving he that receiveth it.

So, how about those Seattle Seahawk Super bowl winners? A young team, a coach who wasn't even considered by many as NFL material, a quarterback drafted in the 5th year without a "premiere" status label... Looks like the odds are stacked up against them, right? What happened? Together, they took advantage of every opportunity with their "can-do positive attitude", overcame every obstacle, and found themselves as the Super bowl XLVIII champs! That Vince Lombardi trophy was proudly paraded through the streets of Seattle on Wednesday February 5, 2014.

I'm sure you've had one! A victory that is...Just think of when you're a baby...Not only can't you walk... you can't talk yet, you can't walk yet, and you can't even feed yourself. Now look where you are! How you've grown! All that you've learned!

Now can you think of something that you've had to overcome? Could be anything: physical, emotional, intellectual, financial, relational.... Write it down here:

_____

_____

When I was in junior high I wanted to try out for a role as a drill team leader. This required my own made-up dance routine to music to display in front of an audience of judges and onlookers. I knew nothing about creative dance at the time and it really showed when I tried out! I clumsily fumbled through the whole routine. I felt miserable. But I didn't give up. Luckily, I still found myself happily following my new instructors as a drill team member for the next year. With these new skills I tried out for cheerleading the next year and made it to my surprise and delight.

Let's take a look at the life of Jacob in the Bible. Jacob, whose name means "deceiver" was the second-born of a set of twins. The first-born was given all the privileges and blessings in their "birthright." This birthright was entitled to his older brother Esau. One day Jacob tricked Esau into selling him his birthright over a bowl of soup. Esau swore to sell it to him saying... "What good is it to me?" And his destiny was altered forever. Jacob not only tricked Esau out of his birthright his mother helped him to dress up as Esau to inherit the blessing his father Isaac desired for his

SON ESaU. WHEN ISaac, HIS FatHeR, SpokE HE KNEW tHat HE couLd NOt take HIS WordS back tHat HE bLeSSed Jacob WitH. THIS Made ESaU, WHo WaNted HIS FatHeR'S bLeSSiNg So aNgry, HE WaNted to coMe aFter Jacob.

WeLL Jacob eScaped aND aLoNg tHe Way gueSS WHat HappeNed? aLL HIS LiFe HE eNcouNtered SituatioNS WHere peopLe Were deceivíNg HiM. You caN read about tHIS StartiNg iN GeNeSIS 28. HIS uNcLe deceived HiM over HIS WageS aNd HIS WiveS. HIS cHILdreN deceíved HiM. aN iMportaNt LeSSoN iN SoWiNg aNd reapiNg. aNyWay, God'S HaNd oF grace WaS upoN Jacob. Jacob WaS gíveN Witty iNveNtioNS iN dreaMS, HE cLuNg to tHe proMiSeS oF God oN HIS LiFe, aNd Jacob Had MuLtipLe eNcouNterS WitH tHe Lord. At oNe poiNt eveN Jacob WreStLed WitH tHe aNgeL oF tHe Lord aLL NigHt LoNg. Jacob WreStLed aNd Said "I WiLL Not Let tHee go, eXcept tHou bLeSS Me."

THe aNgeL Said... "WHat iS tHy NaMe?" aNd Jacob Said, "Jacob." aNd iN GeNeSIS 32:28 We read...

"aNd He Said, THy NaMe SHaLL be caLLed No More Jacob, but ISraeL: For aS a priNce HaSt tHou poWer WitH God aNd WitH MeN, aNd HaSt prevaiLed." iN SoMe verSioNS oF tHe BibLe We read... Jacob "caMe tHrougH" (MeSSage), "StruggLed aNd WoN" (CEB), aNd "overcaMe" (NIVUK), (OJB).

So Jacob, the Father of the twelve tribes of Israel, son of Abraham and Isaac, received a new name and was blessed to be a blessing. How did he start...With the name "deceiver."

Were there trials along the way? Yes. Did he face consequences for his mistakes? Yes. Was it a one-time victory for Jacob? No. Did he believe in God's promises? Yes. Did God fulfill his plans for his life? Yes. Jacob had to fight. He fought on God's side and he overcame.

In this life we have some overcoming to do! Why? Because we are pilgrims in this world.... Just passing through. This isn't "It" for us. Life is but a vapor that appears and then vanishes. Eternity is forever, however. Think of it. You have free-will and make choices every day. It would be wise if you began to ask God now... Psalm 90:12... "So, teach us to number our days, that we may apply our hearts unto wisdom."

So, how do we do it? With Jesus in our boat! What was the Lord Jesus "overcome" with? "Pity." For he saw the sick and had compassion on them. Matthew 14:14 (Message) Read and write down James 5:11 here:

_____

_____

_____

_____

When you are in Christ you've got EVERYTHING you need and you can handle everything that comes your way! So hold on to Christ! And what is the prize? Jesus! And what is the reward? Read and write down James 1:12 here:

_____

_____

_____

Blessings and Life...WOW! Think of it. The Bible says that your eyes haven't seen, your ears haven't heard, and your mind can not even imagine how good it is, what God has in store for those who love Him.

So overcoming... this is God's upper-deck perspective for you. Do you need courage? Ask for it. Is there an opportunity in front of you God wants you to pursue? Lay hold of it! Is there a challenge you're currently facing that's trying to rob you of your peace? Fight for it! The Joy of the Lord is your strength! You can persevere. Remember God's promise in Jeremiah: "I have a hope and a future for you!" (Jeremiah 29:11) Has God given you a promise in His Word pertaining to your life? Stand on it! And don't get deceived! God does not change. He is only good!

Day 14

What is JESUS Looking For?

Luke 18:8b... Nevertheless When the Son of Man cometh, Shall He Find Faith on the earth?

What is God pleased With? Our Faith! Over and over in the New Testament Jesus states it is because of your Faith... it Will be done... you Will be Healed... this Mountain Will be Moved. That you take up the Shield of Faith (Jesus, your portion) and arm yourselves With the Full armor of God; that the just Man Shall Live by His Faith (Hab 2:4); that He is praying your Faith Would Not Fail (Luke 22:32); that your Faith Has Saved you (Luke 7:50).

What is your Faith? Your belief that: God is good and What He Says is true! Hebrews 11:1 Says... "Now Faith is the Substance of things Hoped For, the evidence of things Not Seen. Those on the old testament all died in Faith, Not having received the promises, but having Seen them aFar off, and Were persuaded of them, and embraced them, and confessed that they Were Strangers and pilgrims on the earth. (Hebrews 11:13) And... verse 16 Says... they desire a better country, that is an Heavenly: Wherefore God is Not ashamed to be called their God: For He Hath prepared For them a city.

So What Should you do? The Lord calls us to Stand in our Faith. Get alone With the Lord and His WORD and Find out What personal promises He is Making For your Life and to your circumstances and then Stand in Faith on those promises. Ephesians 6:13 Wherefore take unto you the Whole armour of God, that ye May be able to Withstand in the evil day, and having done all, to Stand. And vs. 16 Above all, taking the Shield of Faith, WhereWith ye Shall be able to quench all the Fiery darts of the Wicked.

The Story of Luke 18:1-8 is a parable Jesus tells us to alWays pray and not to Faint;

Read Luke 18:1-8

Write out verses 7-8

_____

_____

_____

_____

_____

_____

_____

_____

_____

God loves you so much. He's listening to your prayers because you are His child He says..... In Matthew 17:20 "If you have faith as a grain of mustard seed, ye shall say unto this mountain, remove hence to yonder place; and it shall remove; and nothing shall be impossible unto you." If you've ever seen a mustard seed it is REALLY, REALLY, Really small.

Now read the story of the Centurion in Matthew Ch. 8 who had Great Faith.

Read Matthew 8:5-13

Write out vs. 8-9

_____

_____

_____

_____

_____

_____

_____

Why did Jesus Marvel?

_____

_____

I pray that as you seek the Lord in all your ways you will cause Jesus to marvel at your faith because your heart, attitudes, actions, and choices are in accordance with that good and acceptable and perfect will of God. Jesus is your answer!

PS. Remember ... the story of Jesus in the boat with His disciples sleeping... The winds blew the rains came, the boat rocked. There was a terrible storm and those disciples were afraid. So they woke Jesus up and what did they say... "Lord, save us: we perish." What did Jesus say ... "Why are ye fearful, O ye of little faith?" Then He arose, and rebuked the winds and the sea; and there was a great calm. Those disciples marveled at Jesus. They said... "What manner of man is this, that even the winds and the sea obey Him!" Friends, God speaks.... And it IS. Commit your way to the Lord, to know Him, His voice, His will and trust in His Lordship. He's Trustworthy, and wants to prove it to you!

Write your own prayer of dedication here:

_____

_____

_____

_____

_____

_____

_____

_____

_____

_____

_____ **AMEN!**

Instructions For Readers and Discussion Leaders

1) Have a Bible and pen available at the beginning of each lesson.

2) IF readers are new to the Scriptures inform them of the index at the beginning of their Bibles which will lead them to chapter and verse.

3) After individual meditation on the day's lesson, an open discussion in the group led by the instructor will enhance learning.

4) IF you are the teacher spend time in advance reviewing the days lesson and applications to your own life. This will enhance the discussion process.